This book belongs to:

____

Made in United States
Orlando, FL
11 April 2022

16728114R00065